The Road to Amazing

Finished
7-10-16
JS

# THE BASICS

The
BASICS

# *The* ROAD *to Amazing*

## basics of christian practice

**Clayton Oliphint**
*and*
**Mary Brooke Casad**

Abingdon Press
Nashville

**The Road to Amazing**
**Basics of Christian Practice**

*Copyright © 2016 by Abingdon Press*
All rights reserved.

*This book is printed on elemental chlorine-free paper.*
ISBN 978-1-5018-1313-9

16 17 18 19 20 21 22 23 24 25—10 9 8 7 6 5 4 3 2 1
MANUFACTURED IN THE UNITED STATES OF AMERICA

To our families:

**(Clayton)** Lori, Erin, Katy, Grant

**(Mary Brooke)** Vic, Carter, McCrae, Melissa,
Revol, Patrick, Ana—

Each of you, in your own way,
makes the road we walk amazing!

# CONTENTS

# About the Authors

**Clayton Oliphint** and **Mary Brooke Casad** are siblings who share a passion for discipleship and helping others grow as followers of Jesus Christ. They grew up in four United Methodist congregations in Louisiana and Texas where their father, the late Ben Oliphint, was pastor. Following his election to the episcopacy in 1980, he served the Topeka and Houston areas. Both Clayton and Mary Brooke are married to fellow "preacher's kids" who share their rich heritage of faith and ministry.

**Clayton** is senior pastor of First United Methodist Church in Richardson, Texas, a church of six thousand members. He received his undergraduate degree from Austin College and a Master of Divinity and Doctor of Ministry from Perkins School of Theology. He and his wife, Lori, are the parents of three children. Beyond his church and local community involvement, he serves on the steering committee of the Office of Christian Unity and Interreligious Relationships of The United Methodist

Church, and as a director of the Texas Methodist Foundation Board.

**Mary Brooke** is former Executive Secretary of the Connectional Table of The United Methodist Church. She served as Director of Connectional Ministries in the Dallas area from 1997 to 2007. Currently, she is a trustee and past chair of the Foundation for Evangelism and a director of the Texas Methodist Foundation Board. She has a degree in journalism from Southern Methodist University and is the author of several *Bluebonnet the Armadillo* children's books, written to teach Texas children about their rich local heritage. She and her clergy husband, Vic, have two sons, a daughter-in-law, and three grandchildren. They live in Sulphur Springs, Texas.

Clayton and Mary Brooke are coauthors of The Basics series. Drawing on their rich faith heritage, they write with a warm storytelling approach that resonates and helps make practical connections between faith and action.

# INTRODUCTION

For many centuries, the word *journey* has been used when describing the life of a follower of Jesus. It is a word that helps us understand that being a Christian is not reaching a fixed point—rather, we are walking the road that leads to salvation and freedom, striving to follow the example of Christ. The journey is not always smooth or easy, but it is filled with remarkable moments of insight and blessing. Along the way, Jesus shows up and surprises us. He is our traveling companion, walking the road with us, even when we are not aware of his presence.

Each summer, the church Clayton pastors hosts a Vacation Bible School in an apartment complex close to the church campus. Most of the children come from homes where the parents do not speak English as their first language. One summer, the theme of the VBS was Bible stories. Each day featured a different story from the Bible: Jacob and Esau, David and Goliath, Jesus multiplying the loaves and fishes, and Jesus on the road to Emmaus. On the last day of the school, the teachers asked the children, "What was your favorite story that you learned this week?" Some said, "I liked David and Goliath." Some said, "I liked the one about the loaves and fishes." Others said, "I liked Jacob and Esau." But one little boy raised his hand and said, "My favorite is that story about the road to amazing. It is the story of faith for me."

That little boy had remarkable insight. The journey with Jesus is truly "the road to amazing"! Beginning at our baptism, this journey with Jesus takes us to unexpected places. We must decide who this Jesus is and what he is all about. If Jesus is the Messiah, what implications does this have for our lives? What does it mean for us to follow him on this amazing journey?

The journey is also a pathway to transformation. As we walk this road of faith, we are constantly challenged to grow in God's grace. This transformation means taking a hard look at our lives and values, and casting off those things that do not reflect or embody the love of God. It also means that as we walk with Jesus we confront injustice and spiritual forces of wickedness at work in the world.

What makes this road so amazing? Where do we begin? God has so loved the world in general, and each of us in particular, that God gave us the gift of God's only Son (John 3:16). This gift is pure grace. And as we know so well from one of the most popular hymns ever, God's grace is amazing!

We hope you will find encouragement for your journey as you encounter Jesus on the road to amazing.

**—Clayton Oliphint** and **Mary Brooke Casad**

# HOW TO USE THIS BOOK

*The Road to Amazing* is one of three small-group studies in The Basics, a discipleship series that explores the basics of living as a follower of Jesus. Each study may be done separately or as part of a twelve-week course. Some congregations may choose to use one or all three studies in a churchwide study series.

This book is designed for you, the group member. Each week you will read one chapter and then gather with your group for discussion. (A leader guide with session outlines and other helps is available separately.) If desired, you also may use this book as a personal devotion guide. Before reading each chapter, offer a prayer and invite God's presence and wisdom as you seek to follow Jesus on the road to amazing.

Our approach throughout is to write on a very personal and practical level, speaking with a unified voice except when sharing our individual stories (these are identified by our names, which appear in bold within parentheses). Our hope is that as you read you will feel you are traveling with friends who are making the journey along with you.

Each chapter begins with a passage of Scripture, followed by several short thematic readings. At the end of the chapter, you will find a Reflect section where you can record your thoughts in response to specific questions. Drawing on the imagery of a road trip, you will be guided by the following:

## Historical Marker

Historical markers are plaques or signs found in particular locations that commemorate events or persons of historic interest. For our purposes, we will use the term *historical marker* to indicate the study of Holy Scripture. The Bible is full of places, events, and people who have shaped our understanding of God for thousands of years. It's the starting place on the road to amazing!

Each chapter is based on a passage of Scripture, which is printed at the beginning of the chapter. The Historical Marker section invites you to reflect further on the Scripture passage.

## Points of Interest

A *point of interest* is a term used to describe interesting and useful locations on maps. It may include geographical landmarks as well as places providing lodging, food, gas stations, or entertainment. This section invites you to reflect on the insights you gained from each section of the chapter and to note specific points that are significant for you. Surely there are many points of interest along the road to amazing!

##  Souvenir

A road trip would be incomplete without a souvenir! *Souvenirs* are items we keep as reminders of particular events, places, and people. This section invites you to share what is most memorable about the chapter. Was it a passage of Scripture, a story, or a statement? This is an opportunity to write down your main take-away from the chapter.

Your responses to these prompts will help you make personal application and prepare you for sharing with your small group.

As you make your way through this book—whether you are reading it as part of a small-group study or as a personal devotion guide—we hope you will find encouragement and inspiration for your discipleship journey along the road to amazing!

CHAPTER 1

# BAPTISM

The Journey Begins

*Now when all the people were baptized, and when Jesus also had been baptized and was praying, the heaven was opened, and the Holy Spirit descended upon him in bodily form like a dove. And a voice came from heaven, "You are my Son, the Beloved; with you I am well pleased."*

*(Luke 3:21-22)*

## CHAPTER 1

# BAPTISM

## The Journey Begins

Every journey begins with a first step. The term *journey* has been appropriately used across the centuries to describe what the Christian faith is all about. As believers, Jesus has invited us into a life of faith and trust. It is a journey filled with exciting discoveries about ourselves, our world, and especially about the remarkable God who travels with us. It is also a journey on which we experience disappointment, pain, and suffering. The road is not always easy, especially as we begin to look at the plight of our neighbors and realize that their challenges are also our own. The good news is that the One who invites us into the journey will be with us on the journey.

Ultimately, it is a road that leads to amazing—both in the quality of our lives, in the here and now, and in the promise of what is to come.

In order to begin this journey, it is good to first take stock of your life. Ever look in a mirror and not like what you see? Some of us stare at the image reflected back at us and begin to pick it apart. Too fat, too skinny, eyebrows too thin, eyebrows too thick, too many freckles, too many wrinkles, too much hair, not enough hair. On and on the list goes as we beat ourselves up for what we are *not*. Then we compare ourselves, often unfavorably, to others. We spend way too much of our energy and attention focused on these perceived negatives about our lives, which only serves to bring us down. We can get so consumed with our own needs and desires that we become quite self-absorbed. We don't want to be selfish people, but there's something about our nature that can be pretty selfish. At times we become the center of our own universe. As it turns out, this is a common human problem—it's called sin.

You may not like what you see in the mirror. You may think, "I can't see myself differently than I have always seen myself, and it's too late to see myself any other way. I have lived my life this way too long to change now."

But change can be revolutionary! For example, history tells us there was a time when people believed that the earth was the center of the universe and the sun and the moon revolved around the earth. But then Copernicus introduced a new theory, also championed by Galileo, that the sun is at the center of our solar system and the earth and moon orbit around the sun. It was a revolutionary change in how our world and universe were viewed.

Back to the mirror. What if you saw yourself and your life differently? Instead of you in the center and everyone else, including God, revolving around you, what if a revolutionary shift was made in your life? What if you put God at the center? What if you understood that God is the center and that you and others move in relationship to God? What kind of difference might that make in your life?

If we can embrace that view, then when we look in the mirror we are not just consumed with our own desires, our own interests, our own problems, our own dreams, and our own hang-ups. Instead we see ourselves as people who are in relationship with God. God is the source of our strength. We are children of God and loved by God. But we are not at the center; God is at the center. As Christians, this change of perspective is a revolutionary life change. It's the beginning of a journey with Jesus on the road to amazing! And it all begins in baptism.

# Why Is Baptism Important?

Baptism is the beginning point for believers on the amazing journey of faith. Why is baptism so important? First, it was important for Jesus and the early church. As we read in Luke 3:21-22, Jesus was baptized. Then he commanded his disciples: "Go therefore and make disciples of all nations, baptizing them in the name of the Father and of the Son and of the Holy Spirit" (Matthew 28:19).

On the Day of Pentecost, Peter encouraged those who would respond to the good news of the story of Jesus to "Repent, and be baptized every one of you in the name of Jesus Christ so that your sins may be forgiven; and you will receive the gift of the Holy Spirit" (Acts 2:38). He reminded them that this promise was for all of them and for their children. That very day three thousand were baptized and added to the church (the first megachurch). Throughout the Book of Acts we see that, as the disciples went into the world, they invited people to believe in Jesus. Day after day the Lord added to the number of those responding, and as they responded they—and sometimes their entire households, as was the case for Lydia in Acts 16:15 and the jailer in Acts 16:33—were baptized. Established in Scripture and lived out in tradition, the sacrament of baptism marks initiation or entry into the household of faith at whatever age it is received. It is the beginning of an amazing journey.

**(Mary Brooke)** Like many other pastors, my husband, Vic, officiates at numerous baptisms of people of all ages. But perhaps one of the most memorable was the baptism of a ninety-year-old man. Surrounded by his family, who had come to celebrate both his ninetieth birthday and his baptism, this man knelt at the altar, took the baptismal vows, heard his name called, and felt the baptismal waters on his head. Several members of the Sunday school class he had been attending for months also stood beside him to welcome him as a new member of Christ's church. One is never too young or too old to join the journey on the road to amazing!

# Claimed by God

When Jesus was baptized, the Holy Spirit descended, "And a voice from heaven said, 'This is my Son, the Beloved, with whom I am well pleased'" (Matthew 3:17). When we are baptized, this is God's message to each of us: "This is my beloved son or daughter, with whom I am well pleased." Your baptism tells you that you are a child of God who has been claimed by God. It is not because of anything you have done to deserve this title; it is a gift of God's grace.

**(Clayton)** Several years ago, a family joined our church. Their young adult son had special needs due to a genetic disorder that left him with an inability to speak, walk, or do almost anything. As his mother liked to say, what he could do was receive and give love. When we talked together about them joining the church, the parents shared that they had been baptized, and their other children had been baptized also. But their son with special needs had never been baptized. They had been told in another church he was ineligible to be baptized because he couldn't take the baptism vows. We explained that our understanding of baptism was different—that our emphasis was on what God was doing in claiming us in baptism. We arranged for him to be baptized a few weeks later in our Sunday morning worship service. When we asked him the questions that are part of the baptism vows, the congregation answered on his behalf as we proclaimed the truth he had been claimed by God as a child of God. There was not a dry eye in the house. It was a beautiful reminder to all of us that baptism is not about our worthiness or our ability but about God's grace.

God's grace is present in our lives before we are even aware of it. Through this grace God has initiated a relationship with us. It is what theologians call prevenient grace, the grace that precedes our understanding and our decisions. This is the grace that nudges us toward a relationship with God by prompting our spirit, convicting us of our shortcomings and sinfulness, and leading us toward accepting a relationship with God. It reminds us that God claims us before we claim God. This is one reason the age of the person being baptized is not as important as is the emphasis on God, who in this sacrament offers a relationship to us. At what age can we ever comprehend such a gift? The God of this universe, who created everything that is, desires a personal relationship with each of us! Is that not amazing?

**(Clayton)** When I was in seminary studying theology, our class asked our professor, retired United Methodist Bishop William McFerrin Stowe, about the concept of God's preceding, or prevenient, grace. He explained it in theological terms, and I think he noticed that all of our heads were spinning, so he told us a story.

God's grace
is present in our lives
before we are even
aware of it.

When he and his wife, Twila, had been married for a time, they found out that they were expecting their first child. They were so excited! For nine months they waited, prepared the nursery, and dreamed of what this child would be. Their hearts were full of love for this child before they had ever seen the child. In the ninth month, Twila went into labor, and they went to the hospital. But something had gone wrong. The child, a beautiful baby girl, was stillborn. They were devastated, as you can imagine. They grieved and cried and held each other, their hopes and dreams shattered. After they got back home, they went into the nursery they had prepared for their child. As they embraced, Twila looked up at her husband and said, "My arms literally ache to hold that child." Bishop Stowe finished the story and said to us, "Now do you understand prevenient grace? Do you understand that God's arms literally ache to hold each one of you? That's how much God loves you." I doubt that anyone who heard Bishop Stowe's description of grace has ever forgotten it.

In baptism, "child of God" becomes your primary identity. We have lots of identifiers: male, female, brown, white, black, nationality, rich, poor, and on and on. But our primary identity through baptism is "child of God." It's important when you look in the mirror that you understand this. No, you're not the center of this universe, but there is a God who is at the center of all life. There is a God at the center of this world who has claimed a relationship with you and sees you as God's own beloved child. The Old Testament tells us we were fearfully and wonderfully made (Psalm 139:14)—every one of us. Fearfully and wonderfully made!

You were made by God, and you are created in the image of God. When you look in the mirror, begin to see yourself and treat yourself as a child of God. You are important to God. God loves you. That's one of the most basic affirmations of our faith. In the waters of baptism, we receive the gift that God has claimed us as God's children. You are a child of God. This is a reminder of God's prevenient grace, the grace that precedes our awareness or our response. It is God initiating a relationship with us. The emphasis in baptism is not on the worthiness of the believer but on the goodness of God. It is recognition of what God has done, is doing, and will do in the life of the baptized.

There are practical ways you can remember your baptism. Sometimes there are moments in worship when we are invited to remember our baptisms and be thankful. This may involve touching water as a physical act of remembering. But in everyday life we can also remember. When we shower or bathe and feel the water on our skin, we can have a daily reminder that through the waters of baptism we have been claimed by God and given an identity. When it rains, it a good reminder that, just as God washes and cleanses the earth, so God also washes and cleanses our hearts and souls. When he faced doubt, darkness, and discouragement, Martin Luther used to put his hand on his head as a way to give himself courage and strength, and he would shout out against the darkness, "I have been baptized!"[1]

In baptism,
"child of God"
becomes your
primary identity.

**(Clayton)** At the church I serve, when we baptize a person at any age, we always remind them that baptism gives them an identity as a child of God. Sometimes in life we forget who we are and lose our identity. We remind the newly baptized that they are not only baptized; they are baptized into a community of faith. That church community, and the family and friends who surround them, will be there all along their journey in life to remind them who they are—a child of God. Our choir often sings a beautiful response, a chorus by Layton De Vries: "O child, child of God, rest assured, the Lord is with you."[2] Indeed, God is with us on this road to amazing that begins in baptism!

# Forgiven

Baptism teaches us that we are forgiven. Luke tells us that John the Baptist "went into all the region around the Jordan, proclaiming a baptism of repentance for the forgiveness of sins" (Luke 3:3). Forgiveness, the cleansing of our hearts, is what the water is about. It's an outward and visible sign of the cleansing God is doing on the inside through grace. How much water does it take to wash us clean? That has been debated among Christians for centuries. Far too much time is wasted in heated discussion about immersion versus sprinkling or pouring. The main thing to focus on is the gift that God offers to us in our baptism—an identity as a child of God who has been forgiven.

You are forgiven! Have you ever looked in the mirror and claimed that? Some people don't realize they need to be forgiven. Some people don't believe they can be forgiven. The Bible is clear: we *all* are sinners, and *all* stand in need of forgiveness. We all have sinned and fallen short of the glory of God, as Paul tells us in Romans 3:23. But the Bible is also clear that God is a forgiving God. And our baptism is a reminder of God's gift of forgiveness. There is nothing you have ever done that God is not willing to wash clean. As 1 John 1:9 reminds us, "If we confess our sins, he who is faithful and just will forgive us our sins and cleanse us from all unrighteousness."

Our God is a forgiving God. Baptism is a reminder that our sins have been washed away and we have a clean slate to start over. What a blessing to see ourselves as children claimed by God, loved by God, and forgiven by God.

**(Clayton)** When I was starting out in ministry, I went to see a church member in her mid-eighties who was near death. When I arrived, she asked her family to step out of the room for a minute. She wanted to share with me her concerns that she could never be forgiven for something she had done in her early twenties. It was really bothering her, and she was not sure if she would go to heaven. I shared with her that God is a God of forgiveness, and I told her of the assurance we find in Scripture that as she confessed her sin, God would forgive. We prayed and we both cried as God's amazing grace was present in that space as she truly knew and accepted that her sins had been forgiven. But what really got me was that she had been sitting in church pews her whole life, hearing a message about a God who forgives, but had never, until that moment, come to grips with the truth that she was forgiven. Have you?

Realizing you are forgiven has implications for how you live your life. Having been forgiven, we are called to forgive others. On a practical level, this may be one of the most challenging aspects of living a Christian life. In Matthew's Gospel we read the story of Peter asking Jesus about forgiveness: "Then Peter came and said to him, 'Lord, if another member of the church sins against me, how often should I forgive? As many as seven times?' Jesus said to him, 'Not seven times, but, I tell you, seventy-seven times'" (Matthew 18:21-22).

Seventy-seven times? What is Jesus talking about? To complicate matters further, some of the ancient manuscripts say "seventy times seven times." Not just seventy-seven, but four hundred and ninety times! Whether by addition or multiplication, this forgiveness business is a complicated formula.

Some have suggested that Jesus wasn't being literal when he gave those numbers, that he was using the numbers as a way of saying to Peter, "Keep working at forgiveness until you get it right." Many times we think we have forgiven someone but we keep replaying the tapes of what that person has done to us, and the bitterness we feel toward her or him lingers. Maybe our forgiveness is not yet complete. Perhaps this is what Jesus was suggesting to Peter—that forgiveness is a process you have to work out over time. Forgiving is not forgetting. It does not mean condoning or accepting what a person has done to you. It is more about not allowing the act that was done to you to have power over your life. Rather than living with bitterness, which sometimes can possess us to the point of being overwhelmed, we choose to forgive. In the process we find great freedom for living.

We are on a journey with Jesus. When we hold on to wrongs that have been done to us, it slows us down and takes our focus off of the One who has forgiven us of our sins. In teaching his disciples to pray, Jesus reminded them of the importance of forgiveness:

> *And forgive us our sins,*
>     *for we ourselves forgive everyone indebted to us.*
> *And do not bring us to the time of trial.*
>                                           *(Luke 11:4)*

We forgive because we have been forgiven. Our baptism is a powerful reminder of this truth. Every time we remember our baptism, we are claiming this truth: our sins have been forgiven! On this road to an amazing life with Jesus, we are called to do the same.

## Spirit-led

In baptism we are given an identity as children of God who have been forgiven by God. Our baptism also helps us recognize that our lives are being led by the Holy Spirit. In baptism we have been adopted by God. As the

Apostle Paul wrote: "For all who are led by the Spirit of God are children of God. For you did not receive a spirit of slavery to fall back into fear, but you have received a spirit of adoption. When we cry, 'Abba! Father!' it is that very Spirit bearing witness with our spirit that we are children of God" (Romans 8:14-16).

You are a spiritual being. You are a spiritual person. You have a source of strength beyond yourself. You are not left helpless and hopeless. There is a God who is at the center of this universe.

Seeing God in the proper perspective means we understand that we are not in charge of empowering our lives, but there is a God who gives us strength and empowers our lives. There is a God who is leading us. The Spirit of the living God, the Spirit of Jesus Christ, is alive and is empowering our lives. We are blessed with a strange and amazing sense of calm, peace, and comfort in the midst of our storms. The Spirit stirs us as we see the plight of our brothers and sisters. The Spirit convicts us as we see people, who are also children of God, living in conditions in which they are not being treated as children of God. This means it is incumbent upon us to hold up those mirrors to the world and proclaim: "Look! This is wrong! This is wrong because these are children of God. You can't treat people like that who are children of the King." The Spirit is giving us strength so that each one of us can use our gifts and talents to make a difference in the world. In a sense, your baptism is your ordination into ministry. Every baptized Christian is called to be a minister of the good news.

The baptismal waters are an outward and visible sign of the inward grace God has for us. "I'm a child of God, I'm loved, I'm forgiven, and I'm empowered by the Holy Spirit." Look in the mirror and see yourself in a different light. Not as the center of the universe, but as a child of God. The life that you are seeking can never be fulfilled with you at the center. Isn't that ironic? It's only when God is at the center that we can find the true order of life, fulfillment, and blessed purpose. Claim your baptismal identity as a child of God!

**(Mary Brooke)** Clayton and I were both baptized, along with our two brothers, as infants in the churches where our father was the pastor. During that time, a phrase was used in the baptism ritual that has become increasingly meaningful to us. Our parents vowed to "live before these children a life that becomes the Gospel."[3]

Over the years, we've come to understand the power of the double meaning of the word *becomes*. It can be used in the sense of "becoming," such as we would describe an article of clothing that is "becoming" to a person, or to compliment a person whose manners are "becoming" or winsome. Do we live lives that are "becoming" to the gospel of Jesus Christ—lives that reflect we are truly followers of Jesus?

The word *becomes* also can mean to assume the form of, be transformed into, emerge as, mature, metamorphose, turn into.[4] Do we live lives that are being renewed and transformed daily by allowing the Holy Spirit to lead and guide us so that, after a time, we have been sanctified in love and "become" one with Christ Jesus?

We are grateful our parents strove to live lives that reflected both meanings of "becoming the gospel." We are blessed our church families took seriously their vows to "order our lives after the example of Christ, that these children, surrounded by steadfast love, may be established in the faith, and confirmed and strengthened in the way that leads to life eternal."[5] We are disciples of Jesus Christ today because of countless other disciples who nurtured us and continue to nurture us in the resurrection faith!

So the question becomes for each baptized Christian: are we living lives that become the Gospel, so that others might also come to love and serve Jesus?

Take a moment now to do something powerful. Go find a mirror, place your hand on your head, and say these words:

> *I am baptized. God is at the center of my life. I am a child of God. I am forgiven. I am led by the Spirit.*

Do you see yourself in a different light? Do you see your role in the world in a different light? In your baptism, you have been invited to a journey with Jesus on the road to amazing.

*God of new beginnings, thank you so much for inviting me to walk with you on this amazing journey of faith. I am so grateful that you have claimed my life and called me by name. Help me to understand that I am your child: loved by you, forgiven by you, and led by your loving Spirit. Help me* to see others around me as your children also. Open my heart to forgive others as you have forgiven me. Guide me to use my gifts to bless others. O God, what an incredible life you offer to all of us. You have led me to where I am today, and I am confident you have a future for me. What that future holds I do not know, but I trust that you hold the future. Help me to trust as I walk hand in hand with you on this road to amazing. In Jesus' name. Amen.

# REFLECT

## ▧ Historical Marker

Read all four accounts of Jesus' baptism and note the similarities and differences in the space provided:

> *Then Jesus came from Galilee to John at the Jordan, to be baptized by him. John would have prevented him, saying, "I need to be baptized by you, and do you come to me?" But Jesus answered him, "Let it be so now; for it is proper for us in this way to fulfill all righteousness." Then he consented. And when Jesus had been baptized, just as he came up from the water, suddenly the heavens were opened to him and he saw the Spirit of God descending like a dove and alighting on him. And a voice from heaven said, "This is my Son, the Beloved, with whom I am well pleased."*
>
> *(Matthew 3:13-17)*

In Matthew's Gospel, we see that John the Baptist is reluctant to baptize Jesus, saying that he should be baptized by Jesus instead. Jesus encourages John to let it be so for now in order to fulfill righteousness .

> *In those days Jesus came from Nazareth of Galilee and was baptized by John in the Jordan. And just as he was coming up out of the water, he saw the*

> *heavens torn apart and the Spirit descending like*
> *a dove on him. And a voice came from heaven,*
> *"You are my Son, the Beloved; with you I am well*
> *pleased."*
>
> (Mark 1:9-11)

In Mark's Gospel, we have the straightforward story of Jesus being baptized by John without any conversation between the two.

> *Now when all the people were baptized, and when*
> *Jesus also had been baptized and was praying, the*
> *heaven was opened, and the Holy Spirit descended*
> *upon him in bodily form like a dove. And a voice*
> *came from heaven, "You are my Son, the Beloved;*
> *with you I am well pleased."*
>
> (Luke 3:21-22)

In Luke's Gospel, we find a brief statement telling us simply that Jesus was baptized and the Spirit descended on him like a dove. Interestingly, we find this statement after we are told that John the Baptist has been arrested (verse 20), and so only by implication can we assume he was baptized by John.

> *The next day he saw Jesus coming toward him*
> *and declared, "Here is the Lamb of God who takes*
> *away the sin of the world! This is he of whom I*
> *said, 'After me comes a man who ranks ahead of*
> *me because he was before me.' I myself did not*
> *know him; but I came baptizing with water for*
> *this reason, that he might be revealed to Israel."*
> *And John testified, "I saw the Spirit descending*

*from heaven like a dove, and it remained on him. I
myself did not know him, but the one who sent me
to baptize with water said to me, 'He on whom you
see the Spirit descend and remain is the one who
baptizes with the Holy Spirit.' And I myself have
seen and have testified that this is the Son of God."*
(John 1:29-34)

In John's Gospel, John the Baptist is across the Jordan
from where he was baptizing when he is questioned
about who he is, and he acknowledges that the Messiah is
present among them. The next day he identifies Jesus as
the Lamb of God, saying that he saw the Spirit descending
like a dove on Jesus. However, the text does not directly
state that Jesus is baptized.

Similarities:

Differences:

Is there an account of Jesus' baptism that is especially
meaningful to you? Why?

# ☞ **Points of Interest**

What insights did you gain from each section of this chapter?

Why Is Baptism Important?

Claimed by God

Forgiven

Spirit-led

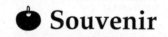 **Souvenir**

What "souvenir" will you take with you as a remembrance of this chapter?

## CHAPTER 2

# DEFINING MOMENTS ON THE JOURNEY

Once when Jesus was praying alone, with only the disciples near him, he asked them, "Who do the crowds say that I am?" They answered, "John the Baptist; but others, Elijah; and still others, that one of the ancient prophets has arisen." He said to them, "But who do you say that I am?" Peter answered, "The Messiah of God."

He sternly ordered and commanded them not to tell anyone, saying, "The Son of Man must undergo great suffering, and be rejected by the elders, chief priests, and scribes, and be killed, and on the third day be raised."

Then he said to them all, "If any want to become my followers, let them deny themselves and take up their cross daily and follow me. For those who want to save their life will lose it, and those who lose their life for my sake will save it. What does it profit them if they gain the whole world, but lose or forfeit themselves? Those who are ashamed of me and of my words, of them the Son of Man will be ashamed when he comes in his glory and the glory of the Father and of the holy angels. But truly I tell you, there are some standing here who will not taste death before they see the kingdom of God."

(Luke 9:18-27)

## CHAPTER 2

# DEFINING MOMENTS ON THE JOURNEY

The journey with Jesus on the road to amazing has some points along the way that are moments of decision. These are defining moments—moments where we must choose which way we will go and who we will follow. These defining moments have real consequences for our lives. Our choices along the way make the journey rewarding and challenging, and sometimes lead us to a place of real clarity about who we are and what life is all about.

**(Clayton)** When I was a child, I was infected with a disease that continues to plague me to this day—I became a football fan!

It all started when I was eight years old and my father took my brothers and me to our first Louisiana State University football game. Standing there in Tiger Stadium in Baton Rouge, Louisiana, was almost a religious experience. That was especially true the time that Coach Bear Bryant and the Alabama Crimson Tide came to town. Bear Bryant, the famous football coach for Texas A&M and then Alabama, was legendary—his following was almost cultlike. The day that Alabama played LSU, we arrived at the stadium really early so we could be there when Bear Bryant stepped off the bus with his team. When he walked through the crowd, there was a hushed tone. People reached out to see if they could touch the hem of his houndstooth garment. It was like the parting of the Red Sea when he walked through the crowd. Even the LSU fans were in awe of Bear Bryant, although some shouted things at him that were not very nice.

This football fever led me to a love of the game, both as participant and spectator. And if there's one thing I've learned about football, it's this: if you make it to the playoffs, it's win or go home.

## Win by Losing

Win or go home. In any sport, when it comes to playoff time, you win or your season is over and you go home. But in the Christian faith, there is a countercultural motto: "lose or go home." When it comes to Christian faith, the way to win is by losing. This is a crazy countermessage in a world in which many churches talk about maximizing your potential. The "prosperity gospel," as some call it, is about becoming your best self in order to prosper more, increase your territory, and expand your financial wealth. It's all about winning and becoming greater.

But Jesus preaches a very different message than what many of us want to hear. When Jesus' followers realized who he was, they had already been following him. He said to them, "Who do you and the people say that I am?" His disciples replied, "Some say you're another John the Baptist and some say you're another Elijah." He said, "Who do you say that I am?" Simon Peter spoke up and said, "I believe you are the Christ, the Messiah, the chosen one of God." Jesus said to them that the Messiah must suffer and the Messiah must die. Jesus then challenged his disciples and said, "If any want to become my followers, let them deny themselves and take up their cross daily and follow me. For those who want to save their life will lose it, and those who lose their life for my sake will save it" (Matthew 16:13-20, 24, author's paraphrase).

"Lose or go home" is a strange message to a world that preaches fulfilling your potential and becoming a better you. We're bombarded with advertisements about becoming a better person. *Lose weight! Get in shape! Watch your diet! Maximize your potential!* That's the message we hear and respond to.

Our society builds up winners and tears down losers. Sadly, we make a sport of celebrating people as they rise to the top, and then, when they mess up, we as a society seem to delight in watching them fall down. We love to create celebrities and we love to see them fall. You might say that it's a national sport.

As Christians, we are called to a different way of life than just dividing the world into winners and losers. We are called to win by losing. Jesus calls us to deny ourselves. How we respond to Jesus' call becomes a defining moment for each one of us on the journey with Jesus.

## Deny Yourself

"Deny yourself." A life of self-denial? What kind of life is that? Jesus' message is so challenging to us because we have bought into the myth that it's all about us—that it's all about setting our own agenda. And then we hear Jesus' countercultural message, which challenges us to a life of self-denial in which we put Christ first. In other words, we have to give up control. (Anybody else feel squeamish now?)

It means that you are not in control of your life. And don't we all want to be in charge of our lives? That's why it's a struggle to be a follower of Jesus Christ. Christ calls us to get out of the driver's seat and to get into the back seat, to deny that natural impulse to be in charge of our lives. This is why Christianity is such a challenge and sometimes doesn't make sense to us.

You may ask, "Does this mean I can't live out my God-given dreams and potential?" No! You should live out your dreams and potential, but in order to follow Christ, you do so under his terms and not your own. Self-denial is a challenge to us because we want to be in charge. How much did Christ love the church? He spread out his arms and died on the cross for her. So what does it mean to be in charge? Jesus modeled for us what it means to be in charge: you give up control. You let God lead and put yourself in a follower role. You deny yourself in order to follow Christ.

John Wesley, the founder of Methodism, taught a prayer that is helpful in understanding what it means to deny yourself and trust God with your life. It is called "A Covenant Prayer in the Wesleyan Tradition":

> *I am no longer my own, but thine.*
> *Put me to what thou wilt, rank me with whom*
>     *thou wilt.*
> *Put me to doing, put me to suffering.*
> *Let me be employed by thee or laid aside for thee,*
> *exalted for thee or brought low for thee.*
> *Let me be full, let me be empty.*
> *Let me have all things, let me have nothing.*
> *I freely and heartily yield all things to thy*
>     *pleasure and disposal.*
> *And now, O glorious and blessed God,*
> *Father, Son, and Holy Spirit,*
> *thou art mine, and I am thine. So be it.*
> *And the covenant which I have made on earth,*
> *let it be ratified in heaven. Amen.[1]*

Christ calls us
to get out of the
driver's seat, to deny
that natural impulse
to be in charge
of our lives.

**(Clayton)** I recently challenged church members to pray this covenant prayer every day for a month. The feedback our church received was remarkable. Several people reported that praying this prayer had a profound impact on their lives. First of all, the daily discipline of pausing each morning to pray set the tone for their day. Second, many people shared that giving themselves to God like this at the beginning of every morning made them think about how they were yielding their lives to God during the course of each day. One man shared with me, "There were several days I stopped in my tracks and decided not to do something because I had prayed that prayer. I realized that I had to focus each day on what God wanted me to do, and not what I wanted to do." Overall, praying this prayer as a congregation brought a spiritual renewal that was contagious. You might even say it was a defining moment in our congregation's journey.

# Take Up Your Cross

Jesus also told the disciples to "take up [your] cross daily and follow me" (Luke 9:23). The word *cross* in the Greek could mean, in terms of execution by crucifixion, the capital punishment instrument used by the Romans. The Romans, who governed Israel in Jesus' day, crucified people on crossed trees just outside the city limits. When Jesus was probably a young boy of ten to twelve years old, there was a man named Judas the Galilean who led a rebellion against the Romans near the village of Nazareth, where Jesus lived. The Roman authorities quickly suppressed this rebellion, and just four miles from the village of Nazareth, along the roadway between some forests, Roman officials crucified some two thousand or more people as a sign of the cost of messing with Rome. When Jesus set his face to go to Jerusalem, he knew there was a price to pay. He was telling his followers they would need to count the cost of following him and be willing to pay the price.

Now this is the point where many Christians say, "Well, you know, that might have been good for the disciples, but surely Jesus wasn't calling us to do that." To be willing to die for the cause of Christ—is that what Christ is calling us to do?

There have been many who were willing to give their lives in following Christ. In 1939, a young German pastor who was safe and secure in New York City, having fled Nazi Germany, made a momentous decision. He decided that he must go back to Germany and stand up for the Jews who were being systematically killed and persecuted there. Dietrich Bonhoeffer made the decision to leave comfort and safety, to pick up his cross, and to go back to Germany, where he vocally opposed Adolf Hitler and his regime. This decision would cost him his life. He participated in a failed plot to assassinate Hitler, and he was captured and put to death by the Germans in 1945. Dietrich Bonhoeffer's example reminds us of the cost of discipleship, the cost of being a follower of Jesus.

Another follower, Martin Luther King, Jr., had just completed seminary in 1954, when he and his young family moved to Montgomery, Alabama, to pastor a church. Soon, racial tensions drew him into a bus boycott. The other pastors in town approached him and said, "Would you be the leader of our movement, our spokesperson?" King had to weigh the cost to his family, to his church, and to his life. In some of his later writings he talked about that decision, about the struggle in knowing that, if he stepped out in leadership, it would be risky. And it was. His home was bombed several times. He was under constant death threats, and he was ultimately assassinated. All because he stepped out in faith and sought to follow Christ and stand up for the rights of others.

# Daily

Luke 9:18-27 adds a word that is not found in Mark's or Matthew's telling of this story. It is the word *daily* (see Luke 9:23). Matthew and Mark seem to emphasize that we must be willing to put our lives on the line and die for Christ, and Luke surely means this as well. But by adding the word *daily*, he may also be calling us not just to be willing to die for Christ, but also to live daily for Christ.[2] The Greek word *stauros* is translated as "cross." It also means "stake," such as a stake that is stuck in the ground to secure a tent or tether an animal.[3] So Jesus' statement to the disciples could also mean to pull up the stake to which you are tethered, so you can move out of your comfort zone. Pull up your stake, lose your security, and follow Jesus where it is risky. Pull up the stakes that are holding you in a safe place and be willing to risk even life and death to follow Jesus.[4]

So what does it mean for us to take up our cross daily? Most of us are not in a position that we would be martyred for Christ. How can we serve Christ daily in our work, in our families, in our leisure, in our communities? Luke's use of the word *daily* points us to what we do with our lives Monday through Saturday, and not just on Sunday. How we put our faith into practice on a daily basis really becomes defining for who we are as Christ's followers.

**(Mary Brooke)** I saw the reality of living out one's faith exemplified in a powerful way in my childhood. In 1952, when our parents were newlyweds, they started a new church in Monroe, Louisiana. A small group of charter members joined them every Sunday night for Bible study and book reviews of contemporary theologians. The group called itself simply "Sunday Night Study Group."

Over the years, as St. Paul's Methodist Church grew, so did the ties between these couples. Strong friendships were forged through hours of study and prayer as together they struggled with the call of discipleship on their lives in the context of the segregated South. It was this group who stood with our parents during the trying times of the Civil Rights Movement in the 1960s.

Inspired by hearing Martin Luther King, Jr. give a speech in Chicago, our father quoted him in sermons, and the bishop received calls of complaint. Several parishioners wanted Dr. Oliphint moved. I remember our dad saying, when he recounted the story, that the only reason those parishioners could give was that they didn't like his views on civil rights, and the bishop told them that was not grounds for moving a pastor.

Under the Jim Crow laws, an African American could register to vote only with the endorsement of a white person. St. Paul's custodian, a black man named Samuel Tucker, asked our father to go with him to the courthouse to register to vote; so he did. When he returned, a church officer was waiting for our father in the church parking lot.

"Do you see this church that you built?" the man asked, pointing to the building. "Now you're tearing it down, brick by brick."

Soon the bomb threats, harassing phone calls, and letters to the editor in the local newspaper began, followed by a summons to the Louisiana House Committee on Un-American Activity.

And then, one night when our father was meeting with his very supportive district superintendent, my mother called to say there was a burning cross in our parsonage front yard. She later spoke of her gratitude for the district superintendent, who stayed on the phone with her as my father hurriedly drove home.

At the next meeting of the St. Paul's administrative board, a resolution was presented that stated if black persons attempted to worship at the church, they would be given directions to the nearest black church and asked to leave. Our father said if the resolution was approved, he could no longer be their pastor because St. Paul's would have ceased to be a church; it would have become a country club. The board chair, a member of the Sunday Night Study Group, announced there would be a roll-call vote. A motion to table the resolution was quickly made and passed. The meeting adjourned.

The next day, half of the congregation left, taking one-third of the budget with them. "But God provided," our father said. "We had a shortfall of forty thousand dollars, which was exactly the amount we had in the savings account."

Destructive riots began sweeping across many Southern cities, but Monroe city leaders decided to integrate quietly by opening the doors of shops and restaurants to all its citizens. My younger brothers and I were shielded from many of the trials our parents faced, but I remember a period of tension when I was not allowed to answer the telephone, and they moved me to a makeshift bed in my dad's study at the back of the house, out of my front bedroom with the large windows. It would be many years before our dad could talk about this painful time of threats and divisiveness.

Our dad always said it was the pastors who helped bring about civil rights in Louisiana through their brave stances and bold witnesses, supported by many good lay folk. He would tell their stories with great admiration. Many of these pastors were visited by the Ku Klux Klan and harassed as well. Across the years, I've met many "preacher's kids" with stories similar to my own. And over the years, as members of the Sunday Night Study Group began to reassemble at the feet of the Master, and their children gathered for memorial services, the stories have been told again and again. As the daughter of the administrative board chair said of that time, "It was the defining moment of our childhood." We have all agreed that our parents' bold stand was their finest legacy.

St. Paul's is now more than sixty years old and counts persons of color among its membership. Martin Luther King, Jr., who our dad quoted in his sermons to the dismay of some of the church members, now has a national holiday named in his honor. America elected its first African American president. There is much to celebrate about the changes that have taken place in the years since our childhood.

But there is still much to be done. Racial injustice continues to plague our nation and our world. That's why I'm thankful for the many faithful congregations across our world where there are clergy and laity studying God's word together, asking the hard questions of what discipleship means in our day, seeking to live as true followers of Jesus, taking courageous stands in their communities.

May the stories of the faithful who have gone before us continue to embolden us in seeking justice for all God's children.[5]

# What Is Christ Calling You to Do?

What is Christ calling you to do today? It may be easy or it may be hard. Christ calls all of us to a life of self-denial. It's a countercultural call, and not what our society preaches. What would practicing self-denial and taking up your cross to go where Christ leads you mean for you?

Who are the people God is calling you to stand up for and give a voice to their needs? Who's going to stand up for the voiceless if we Christians don't lead? Think about other people in our society who have fallen through the cracks, the people who may feel that they have lost and everyone else has won. They are made to feel as if they are less than others. Christians are called to stand with people in these situations and remind the world that all are precious in God's sight. If you lose yourself in the cause of Christ, you win. Ultimately, it's not about how successful you are, how rich you become, how much you can accumulate, how much power you acquire. To win in life is to learn how to lose, that is, to lose yourself in the cause of Christ. Jesus asks us a hard question: What if, at the end of your life, you realized you had won in all the areas that society says counts for winning, but in so doing you forfeited your life? Christ calls us to lose ourselves for the cause of Christ, and by doing so, we ultimately win.

**(Clayton)** In life, along the way we find people who inspire us to live our lives for Christ. Martin and Rachel were two of the people who really modeled this concept for me. I knew them in their latter years, when they celebrated their seventieth wedding anniversary.

Martin was a kind man who took positions of responsibility within the church throughout his life. But it was the way he lived his faith in action, in the way he treated people, and in the way his faith instructed him to live and give in the world that made so many men want to be the kind of man Martin was.

If you lose
yourself in the
cause of Christ,
you win.

Rachel taught Sunday school for about seventy years, and her passion was helping people grow as disciples. I watched her do this with someone who came to her home to help care for her when she was ill. She said to the young woman, "Will you pray for me?" The young woman responded, "I'm not sure I know how to pray." Rachel said, "Give me your hand. Whatever you need help with, dear, just tell God." And on she went in one of the most beautiful expressions of teaching prayer I have ever witnessed.

After Martin's death, Rachel began to develop dementia, sometimes not knowing her family and those closest to her. One day I stopped by the center where she was living and found her daughter outside her room. She was listening outside the door and her mother was talking. I peered inside the door and saw that Rachel had lined up stuffed animals in chairs. Here in her last days, this woman in her nineties was teaching a Sunday school lesson. Her daughter and I marveled at her command of Scripture as she recalled passage after passage to help her students understand God's love for them. As her daughter said, "She may not remember us right now, but God's Word is so deeply at the heart of who she is. That is what she remembers."

So how can you put your faith into action? This amazing journey with Jesus challenges each one of us to wrestle with what that means for us and to take up the challenge daily. In much of the world it's win or go home. But on this road to amazing, it's all about losing—

losing ourselves in the cause of Christ. As Jesus said, "If you want to be my follower, deny yourself, take up your cross, follow me. If you want to win in life, learn how to lose your life for my sake" (Luke 9:23-24, author's paraphrase). How we respond to that challenge becomes a defining moment for our lives. Those responses often determine whether our road is normal and ordinary, or, as God desires, a road that is extraordinary and amazing.

*Gracious and loving God, today I am challenged by your word. It's not easy for me to think about stepping out of the way and giving you control of my life. I would prefer that you would just bless my agenda for my life. But this day, O Lord, I give myself to you, asking you to direct my steps and my pathway. I recommit my life to you this day. Come into my heart and guide my life. Use me as you will, not as I want. Remind me that I am not in charge; rather, I am following you where you lead. Give me the courage to follow, even if I have to stand up in a way that makes me uncomfortable. I am grateful that you love me and have given your Son for me. Help me to give myself for you. I surrender myself to you. In the name of Christ, my Lord, I pray. Amen.*

# REFLECT

## 🔲 Historical Marker

Reread Luke 9:18-27 ( see page 42).

Luke 9:18–27 is one of the most pivotal passages in Luke's Gospel. The disciples, and all who read this text, are confronted with an important question. After asking the disciples what the crowds are saying about him, Jesus asks, "But who do you say that I am" (Luke 9:20a). It is a question every Christian must answer along the journey of faith. Is Jesus a good man? A prophet? A religious zealot? A political revolutionary? A miracle worker?

Peter answers Jesus quickly and simply: "The Messiah of God" (Luke 9:20b). Messiah is a term that means "anointed one" or "Christ." For centuries the Hebrew people had awaited a Messiah who would restore the kingdom of Israel. The expectation was that the Messiah would be more of a political or military leader. Did Jesus fit the expectation?

Once Peter answers Jesus, the disciples are confronted with what following this Messiah means. They must put their agendas aside, take up their cross daily, and follow Jesus. As we see in Chapter 2 of *The Road to Amazing*, Luke's version of this story adds a word not contained in Mark's and Matthew's versions: daily. Why is this? When Luke writes his Gospel, it has now been some fifty years since the crucifixion and resurrection of Jesus. Earlier writings contain an expectation that Jesus will return any day. Luke's reality is that he has not yet returned, and so people must figure out not only how to be ready to die for Jesus but also how to be ready to live for Jesus on a daily basis. This is at least one thought as to why Luke added this word.

Jesus turns the world's order of priorities upside down with his statement about losing your life in order to save it. Much of the world then—as now—would say, if you want to save your life, then play it safe. Jesus presents a new understanding of what living life is all about. In order to fully experience life, you must learn how to give your life away.

How would you answer Jesus' question, "Who do you say that I am?"

*The son of God. The savior of all mankind.*

---

## ☞ Points of Interest

---

What insights did you gain from each section of the chapter?

Win by Losing

Deny Yourself

Take Up Your Cross

Daily

What Is Christ Calling You to Do?

 **Souvenir**

What "souvenir" will you take with you as a remembrance
of this chapter?

CHAPTER 3

# TRANSFORMING JOURNEY

*[Jesus] entered Jericho and was passing through it. A man was there named Zacchaeus; he was a chief tax collector and was rich. He was trying to see who Jesus was, but on account of the crowd he could not, because he was short in stature. So he ran ahead and climbed a sycamore tree to see him, because he was going to pass that way. When Jesus came to the place, he looked up and said to him, "Zacchaeus, hurry and come down; for I must stay at your house today." So he hurried down and was happy to welcome him. All who saw it began to grumble and said, "He has gone to be the guest of one who is a sinner." Zacchaeus stood there and said to the Lord, "Look, half of my possessions, Lord, I will give to the poor; and if I have defrauded anyone of anything, I will pay back four times as much." Then Jesus said to him, "Today salvation has come to this house, because he too is a son of Abraham. For the Son of Man came to seek out and to save the lost."*

*(Luke 19:1-10)*

## CHAPTER 3

# TRANSFORMING JOURNEY

Our journey on the road to amazing leads us to interesting places and people. These experiences on the journey with Jesus take us to places where, in the light of God's love, we reevaluate our lives. The transformation that begins to take place is sometimes dramatic and sometimes subtle. But make no mistake. If you are traveling with Jesus, you are being transformed.

One of our favorite songs is "Seasons of Love" from the Broadway musical *Rent*. Several years ago we heard it sung at a memorial service, celebrating the lives of clergy and their spouses who had died in the previous year. It was an inspired choice of music. The song talks about the 525,600 minutes that make up each year of our lives and asks the question, "How do you measure the life of a woman or a man?" The beautiful chorus of the song really answers the question: "How about love? / Measure in love."[1]

As the music played, the images of the deceased pastors and their spouses—men and women who had spent their lives sharing God's love—were displayed on video screens. Many of them had helped guide us and had walked with us in joyous moments of celebration. Many of them had been there for us and others through the tragedies of life. Some of them were champions for the underdogs. Some of them were prophetic. All of them were followers of Jesus, and all of them made a profound difference in the world. As their images flashed across the screens, many eyes filled with tears. Yes, the song said it so well. Their lives were, indeed, measured by love.

## Measurements

How do you measure a life? How do you measure happiness? How do you measure success? What are the things you measure that really count? Zacchaeus was one of those people who just somehow got off track in terms of what he measured. When you read that Zacchaeus was small or short of stature, you wonder if this was more than a physical description. Wasn't it also a description of how he felt about himself? Maybe he didn't feel that he measured up in terms of his own life.

Can you visualize Zacchaeus at your high school reunion? Think about a ten-, twenty-five-, or thirty-year high school reunion. In walks Zach, the little guy that everybody picked on. Zach, the least likely to make it in the NBA. Zach, the guy who never could get the girl, was never popular, didn't fit in, and could never measure up because he was small of stature. At least, that's how he felt about himself. So guess who shows up in his own personal helicopter with a wife by his side, flashing his worldly possessions for all to see? It's Zach, showing up to say to everyone, "I'll show you who is small of stature! I'll show you guys how to measure a life."

Zacchaeus must have had a hard life. Something must have happened somewhere along the way. Zacchaeus was missing something and was seeking an answer. He heard about Jesus and he sought out this man. He wanted to see him so badly that when Jesus came to town and the crowds were so overwhelming he couldn't see, Zacchaeus climbed up a sycamore tree.

Where did Zacchaeus go wrong? Maybe it was when he took a job as a tax collector. In biblical times, being a tax collector was not a job for the faint of heart. Tax collectors reported to the Roman authorities. Taxes were collected from the people based on everything they owned and produced. In one sense, much like the taxes we pay today, those taxes were used to fund good roads, the military, and other government benefits. But the Romans were occupying their land, and taxing them beyond what they thought was fair. And Zacchaeus, a fellow Jew, was in cahoots with these foreign invaders. We are told he was rich and had taken more than his share. This was a common practice among tax collectors of that day. Get everything you can from the people, threaten them, and take more. Pay off the Romans with as little as you can and still keep them happy. Keep the rest for yourself.

Sometimes, when feeling small of stature, we feel as though we've got to compensate in some way. Feeling bad about ourselves sometimes makes us do things that we think will make us feel good about ourselves. So Zacchaeus took more and more for himself, and in doing so, became more powerful. But no one liked Zacchaeus, or respected him.

For Zacchaeus, measuring a life seemed to be about wealth and position. As a tax collector, there is no doubt he was an outcast in his community. Maybe it was no accident that he couldn't get a good place on the parade route when Jesus was walking by. Everyone blocked him. Nobody wanted anything to do with Zacchaeus because he was one of "those people." In the eyes of the community, he was in the same category as a prostitute or an adulterer—a sinner they didn't want to be around.

We all know "those people," don't we? Each one of us has our own ideas about "those people," the people we think are beyond the love of God, beyond the love of Jesus. In the Bible, they are called tax collectors, prostitutes, adulterers, Samaritans, Gentiles, and many other names. We know them by different names, depending on where we are and what we have experienced in life. Maybe we're more subtle in our judgment than the religious people in Jesus' day were. Maybe not. It's a common human endeavor to see some people as "less than." It keeps us from looking at our own flaws and deficiencies. We want to crowd these people out of our church. If Jesus came walking through our town, would we rush up to see him and push others out?

But where did Jesus go? Right up to the sycamore tree. Jesus called Zacchaeus down and went to his house. And something happened in that house—something so amazing that when Zacchaeus came out, he said in effect, "Everything that I've done wrong, I want to make it right and then some" (see Luke 19:8). Jesus said salvation had come to his house that day.

## Lost

It's so easy to get "lost" in measuring the wrong things in life. Sometimes we measure ourselves through status, or our position in regards to other people. Sometimes the measurement is financial—have you ever confused your net worth with your self-worth? Sometimes we measure our success by our financial or material success. That measurement, as Zacchaeus found, leaves you empty and lost. You might wake up one day and feel distant from yourself, God, family, and friends, and think, *How did I get here?* Maybe it's because you were measuring your life by things you *thought* would make you happy.

**(Clayton)** Several years ago I told my wife I would take care of paying a bill that was due. I was paying several bills at the time and had them all stacked up in my office, among my piles of files, books, and notes. My wife informed me some weeks later that we had received a notice that our service would be interrupted because we had not paid the bill. I was confident that I had written the check and mailed the bill. I looked over the checkbook and, indeed, I had written the check. I called the business and asked to speak to a customer service representative. He informed me they had not received the check, and I told him that they must have because I had mailed it. I was unable to convince them about how wrong they were and how right I was, so I ended up giving them my credit card information to go ahead and pay the bill.

After hanging up, I started thinking how disorganized their office must be and wondered how many other poor fools were in my position. Then I shifted the blame to the postal service and thought surely someone there hadn't done his or her job. As I was brooding, I shifted some papers on my desk and an envelope fell to the floor. It was the lost bill, which somehow had gotten stuck between two files on my desk. The blame that I had fixed on others for this problem was now squarely back on me. But, as I reasoned, the bill was never really lost; it was just not in the place it was supposed to be!

Many of us end up like my lost envelope. We don't necessarily *feel* lost, but we stop and look up and realize we're not living life the way God would have us live it. Somewhere along the way this realization came to Zacchaeus, and sometimes it comes to us. Thank God that

Jesus loves lost people! If Jesus came to town and went to your house, maybe your neighbors would stand outside like the religious leaders stood outside of Zacchaeus's house, murmuring that he shouldn't have gone in there. But Jesus always goes to find those who have lost their way, to help them find the road that leads to life.

Jesus proclaims at the end of the story: "For the Son of Man came to seek out and to save the lost" (Luke 19:10). The lost—people like us who have measured our lives by other standards. We've searched for meaning and value in other measures, and Jesus came to tell us that we don't have to stay lost—that there's another way that leads to life.

# Truth

There's a moment in the story when Zacchaeus is called down out of his tree, out of his lostness. Jesus said: "I'm going to your house today." So Zacchaeus invited him into his house. Don't you wonder about that dinner conversation?

Perhaps in that conversation Jesus told Zacchaeus the truth about his life. Have you ever had anyone tell you the truth about your life and who you are? Perhaps Jesus said, "You know, Zacchaeus, God loves tax collectors and God also loves the people you're hurting by taking too much of their money. You've been measuring your life in all the wrong ways, Zacchaeus. What you need to know today is that God loves you and will forgive you. Today's the day to turn your life around and start measuring the things that matter."

Zacchaeus found that Jesus was willing to tell him the truth. No doubt, as they shared a meal together in Zacchaeus's home, Jesus spoke the truth in love. "Zacchaeus, why is it that you are stealing from people? Why are you so self-concerned? Why so selfish? Zacchaeus, I am here because you are lost. You are worth something, and it has nothing to do with your money. It has nothing to do with your position. You are worth something to God because God made you."

Every time we open the Bible, Jesus comes into our house. We open the Bible and learn something about who God is, as well as something about who we are. We learn something about the relationship between God and human beings, namely that God loves the lost. God loves the tax collectors. God loves the people hurt by the tax collectors. God doesn't measure life by the stuff that we have. God measures by God's standards. God's love is for everybody. So when God looks at us, God doesn't look at what we have. God looks at who we are.

How does God see you and me? Jesus gives us images of God as a loving parent who sees us as children. We are loved by God. That's the standard of God's measurement—your value comes from God telling the truth about who you are. When Jesus is sitting down in your home as you open your Bible, God is telling you you're God's child and you are loved. That's what creates value; that's how you measure life.

We are loved by God.
That's the standard
of God's measurement—
your value comes
from God telling
the truth about
who you are.

**(Mary Brooke)** One of the reasons we like the story of Zacchaeus so much is because in the story, Jesus shows up as a surprise dinner guest, and we grew up welcoming lots of surprise dinner guests in our home. Our mother frequently invited people over for home-cooked meals, most often following Sunday church services. Her hospitality and culinary skills were legendary. But over the years, what we noticed most was that a diverse group of people dined at her table. We never knew who would be present for a meal. It might be a bishop or a missionary or a star football player; it might be a person who was unemployed and down on his or her luck. It might even be two people she wanted to introduce in hopes of sparking a love interest! It might be a family visiting our church for the first time, or someone who had recently lost a loved one. The one thing that was consistent, however, was the loving way she welcomed each person and made him or her feel special. Everyone received the same gracious treatment; everyone was treated like royalty. We're grateful that our mother modeled Christlike love in treating every person as a beloved child of God!

When Jesus shows up at your house and lets you know you are loved, it's time to get real. You don't have to pretend that you are better than you are. Jesus knows who you are and challenges you to get truthful about who you are. Knowing that you are loved by God, in spite of everything you have done, offers you an opportunity to move forward in a positive direction.

# Salvation

What did salvation mean for Zacchaeus? What does it mean for us? A lot of us think, *Well, after we die, then we get to go to heaven. That's salvation, right?* That's a partially right answer. But the word for salvation is the same word for wholeness in the Greek language. When Jesus said, "Today salvation has come to this house" (Luke 19:9), he was in effect saying, "Today wholeness has happened in Zacchaeus's life." We can be whole in Jesus!

For Zacchaeus, salvation looked like being found. It looked like liberation. It looked like freedom, because he met the Truth and the Truth set him free. He found out the truth about who he was. He was a child of God. That's what gives us value and that's what measures our lives.

Truth set Zacchaeus free—to do what? To give his life away. To say, "I've wronged a lot of people, but I can make it up and live my life differently. I will give half of my goods to the poor, and I will repay anyone I've wronged four times over." The law said that if you stole from someone, you were required to compensate them twice that amount. Zacchaeus doubled the requirement when he said, "Four times I will repay you." He would no longer measure his life by what he could accumulate, but by what he could give.

Measure your life not by what you get but by what you give. What a difference this makes! Getting this right will give you the proper perspective and help you balance your life. By receiving the gift of your value as God's child, you can then understand that your life is an offering. You get to give your life away and share God's love.

**(Clayton)** Some time ago, I was working with a family whose father had died. As a pastor, it is truly one of the highest and holiest experiences to walk with families through death and grief and to plan a meaningful service of worship that is a celebration of faith and life. As we sat down to plan the memorial service, they gave me a copy of the obituary, which contained factual information about the family, the survivors, and an impressive list of professional accomplishments the man had achieved. But as the children and grandchildren began to talk about their father and grandfather, none of the professional accomplishments were mentioned. The conversation was all about the traits of his character. Not once did anyone mention the amount of money in his bank account. Everyone talked about his love and encouragement, his steadfast presence, the wisdom he offered, the integrity he displayed, and the faith that he cherished. It was clear that while all he had accomplished was significant, the life of love he had lived with his family was what really measured up.

Salvation is best understood as a process, rather than a one-time event. The day Jesus came to the home of Zacchaeus was only the beginning of the story, though the Bible doesn't give us any more information about what happened to Zacchaeus after that encounter. Did he continue to reflect upon his experience with Jesus and act upon it? Did he return to his old ways as soon as Jesus left town? Did the impact of Jesus coming into his home continue to affect how he treated the people in his community and how he conducted his business as a tax collector?

What would people say as they look at our lives? Are we living our faith in action? Do we exhibit consistency over time? Has our faith really changed us, or do we put it on when it's convenient?

After an encounter with Jesus, some of us are white hot with zeal for our faith. But sometimes, after a short time, some of us return to our old ways. Others of us may not seem to start off filled with such passion, but the consistency with which we live our lives yields amazing contributions over time.

It's likely that Zacchaeus was so moved by this dinnertime encounter with Jesus that the change that began in him that day continued to develop over time. We don't have further biblical evidence, but many early Christian traditions talk of Zacchaeus as a leader in the early church. It would not be surprising if this were true.

# Transformation

As we journey with Jesus on the road to amazing, something happens to us. It's called transformation. Some of us experience it in a dramatic way; our lives are turned upside down, or more accurately, right side up. Some of us don't really feel any different than we always have in the beginning. But as we begin to examine our lives, we realize that we have changed—following Jesus has shifted our priorities, our actions, and our attitudes.

Theologians call this *sanctification*—the grace that God works in our lives from the time of our acceptance of a relationship with Jesus on through the rest of our lives. God's sanctifying grace shapes and molds us, moving us ever closer to a life aligned with the love of Christ.

**(Clayton)** Several years ago a man came to the church I serve. He had been to church as a child with his grandparents but had never been baptized or confirmed. He had many questions, and was very eager to learn more. He brought his girlfriend to church, and together they were baptized, professed faith in Christ, and joined our congregation. They joined a small group and were excited about growing in their faith. After they had been members about six months, he and I went to breakfast one morning. He said he never really got why going to church and being a Christian was such a big deal to people. He really liked being a part of the church, but he didn't think it would impact the rest of his life so much. But then something happened at his place of employment. Two of his coworkers came to see him one day, closed his door, and said, "We want to know what you've been doing."

"What do you mean?" he said.

They responded, "Over the last few months, something has just been so different about you. You seem so much more positive and productive. We just want to know what you're doing that has changed you so much."

As he sat across the table from me, he looked at me and said, "I had no idea this 'Jesus stuff' would make such a difference in my life. It's amazing!"

Yes, it's amazing. If you spend any time with Jesus, you are bound to see transformation in your life.

God's sanctifying grace
shapes and molds us,
moving us ever closer
to a life aligned
with the love of Christ.

How do you measure a life? It's about love received from God and shared with others. It's as simple—and as complicated—as that. Having been loved, we love. Zacchaeus was lost in his search for meaning, chasing after money, but he found out what really mattered when Jesus told him the truth about who he really was.

Having received love, we are able to give love away. On this road to amazing with Jesus, we don't have to stay lost. Transformation is possible. If it can happen for Zacchaeus, it can happen for us.

*O God, sometimes I struggle to find balance in my life. At times I'm too busy or distracted. And sometimes I'm focused on measuring my life by the wrong things. Come into my home, as you did that day for Zacchaeus, and tell me the truth about who I am and what matters in life. I'm so thankful you love lost people, because that's me. Today I pray that your truth would cut through all the layers of my life and speak to my heart. May salvation come to this house, for the first time, or for the first time in a long time. Bring your sanctifying grace into my life and change me from the inside out. May I begin the work of setting right the wrongs I have committed against others. Open my eyes to see the transformation you are working in my life and in the lives of others. Help me to love "those people" as much as you do, and to see them as brothers and sisters. Teach me to measure life not by stature or wealth, but in love that is received and given through Jesus Christ our Lord. Amen.*

# REFLECT

## ◼ Historical Marker

Reread Luke 19:1-10 ( see page 64).

Luke is the only Gospel that tells the story of Zacchaeus the tax collector, and the transformation that occurs in his life as he encounters Jesus.The story takes place in the city of Jericho, the same city talked about in the book of Joshua, in which Joshua fought the battle of Jericho (Joshua 5:13–6:27). Jesus, whose name is the Greek form of the Hebrew name Joshua, has come to Jericho to tear down the walls built up in the life of Zacchaeus. Luke tells us that Zacchaeus was a chief tax collector and was rich. Tax collectors worked for the Romans, collecting taxes from their own people. Most were known to be corrupt, collecting enough to satisfy the Romans while skimming off the top to fulfill a desire for more wealth. We don't know for sure that Zacchaeus is corrupt until after his meeting with Jesus, when he basically admits it by offering to repay those he has cheated. The law required that the offending party pay back twice as much as was originally taken, but Zacchaeus offers to repay it fourfold, going far beyond what was expected and perhaps proving his guilt and how he felt about it. This story is about the transformation that occurs in his life as he encounters Jesus.

Another part of this story that is interesting to explore is the reaction of the crowd outside the home of Zacchaeus. Jesus has gone to be the guest of someone who is a sinner, and they begin to grumble about it. In biblical times, as today, we like it when Jesus loves and pays attention to people who are obviously good people and deserve to be in his company. But it flies all over us when Jesus offers grace and love to people we believe are not worthy of it. The truth is none of us are worthy of his love and grace, but Jesus offers it anyway.

This passage is a prime example of Luke's desire for all to understand that the love of Jesus is more expansive than the boundaries we set. Jesus has come to seek and save the lost, and we must follow his lead on the road to amazing.

If Jesus came to your house, how would your life be transformed?

## ☞ Points of Interest

What insights did you gain from each section of this chapter?

Measurements

Lost

Truth

Salvation

Transformation

---

## Souvenir

What "souvenir" will you take with you as a remembrance of this chapter?

# CHAPTER 4

# THE ROAD TO AMAZING

Now on that same day two of them were going to a village called Emmaus, about seven miles from Jerusalem, and talking with each other about all these things that had happened. While they were talking and discussing, Jesus himself came near and went with them, but their eyes were kept from recognizing him. And he said to them, "What are you discussing with each other while you walk along?" They stood still, looking sad. Then one of them, whose name was Cleopas, answered him, "Are you the only stranger in Jerusalem who does not know the things that have taken place there in these days? He asked them, "What things?" They replied, "The things about Jesus of Nazareth, who was a prophet mighty in deed and word before God and all the people, and how our chief priests and leaders handed him over to be condemned to death and crucified him. But we had hoped that he was the one to redeem Israel. Yes, and besides all this, it is now the third day since these things took place. Moreover, some women of our group astounded us. They were at the tomb early this morning, and when they did not find his body there, they came back and told us that they had indeed seen a vision of angels who said that he was alive. Some of those who were with us went to the tomb and found it just as the women had said; but they did not see him." Then he said to them, "Oh, how foolish you are, and how slow of heart to believe all that the prophets have declared! Was it not necessary that the Messiah should suffer these things and then enter into his glory?" Then beginning with Moses and all the prophets, he interpreted to them the things about himself in all the scriptures.

*As they came near the village to which they were going,
he walked ahead as if he were going on. But they urged
him strongly, saying, "Stay with us, because it is almost
evening and the day is now nearly over." So he went in to
stay with them. When he was at the table with them, he
took bread, blessed and broke it, and gave it to them. Then
their eyes were opened, and they recognized him; and he
vanished from their sight. They said to each other, "Were
not our hearts burning within us while he was talking to
us on the road, while he was opening the scriptures to us?"
That same hour they got up and returned to Jerusalem;
and they found the eleven and their companions gathered
together. They were saying, "The Lord has risen indeed,
and he has appeared to Simon!" Then they told what had
happened on the road, and how he had been made known to
them in the breaking of the bread.*

*(Luke 24:13-35)*

## CHAPTER 4

# THE ROAD TO AMAZING

How does the "road to Emmaus" turn into the "road to amazing"? Remember the story from the Introduction where the young boy confused the words *Emmaus* and *amazing*? We think he was on to something! The story of the disciples on the road to Emmaus truly is an amazing story of resurrection and new life. The risen Jesus shows up along the way, sometimes just at the time we have lost all hope. Sometimes we don't even know that Jesus has been with us as our traveling companion until we look back later and realize he has been with us all along the way.

**(Clayton)** When our younger brother, Kelley, died at the age of forty-two, we were devastated. A crushing diagnosis of brain cancer had led to month after month of surgeries, chemotherapy, and radiation treatments. In less than a year he was gone, leaving his wife and son, and all of us, with broken hearts. The next few months and years flew by and we often found ourselves in a blur. Some time ago I was speaking with a friend about this tragic time in our lives. He asked the question, "How did you get through it?" I told him that it's still hard to accept to this day, but when you are in the midst of the loss and in the worst of your grief, it's almost surreal. Life and time keep marching forward but you feel stuck, as if life will never be good ever again.

How did we get through it? It was as though Jesus came alongside us and walked us through it. I realize now that it was the prayers of so many people that carried us. Over time, as we came to accept the reality of what had happened and to reflect on his life, we came to have a perspective of profound gratitude to God for having shared life with Kelley. He packed so much life into his short years, and we knew he would want us to move forward with joy. In the light of faith, the day-to-day heaviness of the grief began to fade. Looking back, Jesus was our traveling companion, walking with us down a road that led to new life, new hope, and resurrection. That is the road to amazing!

# The Road to Amazing

Luke is the only Gospel that tells us this Emmaus road story, though Mark's Gospel seems to have knowledge of this story: "After this he appeared in another form to two of them, as they were walking into the country. And they went back and told the rest, but they did not believe them" (Mark 16:12-13). Luke tells us that on that first Easter Day, two of the disciples, one named Cleopas, and the other not mentioned by name, were walking from Jerusalem to a village called Emmaus, about seven miles from Jerusalem. The average modern human being walks about three miles an hour, but these disciples did not have access to the latest and greatest running shoes, and these roads were probably not as smooth as most of the roads we walk. In terrain that was rocky, with hills and valleys, the road was probably twisting and turning and difficult. The walk was at minimum three hours, probably more—a lot of time to ponder what they had just experienced.

One week earlier Jesus had entered Jerusalem. As described in Luke 19, as Jesus rode a colt down from the Mount of Olives into the city, people began spreading their cloaks on the road in front of him. As they approached the city, the whole multitude of disciples joined in and began to praise God "joyfully with a loud voice for all the deeds of power that they had seen, saying, 'Blessed is the king who comes in the name of the Lord! Peace in heaven, and glory in the highest heaven!'" (Luke 19:37-38). The Pharisees were upset by the demonstration and told Jesus to order his disciples to stop. Jesus then said something we all need to remember, pointing to a great truth about the power of God's love: "I tell you, if these were silent, the stones would shout out" (Luke 19:40). God's love will not be silenced.

Yet silence is what the disciples experienced after Jesus was crucified. The events of Holy Week had led to increasing pressure on the religious leaders to do something to stop Jesus. They feared him. He had turned over the tables of the moneychangers in the Temple, forecast the destruction of the Temple, denounced the scribes, and upset the status quo. Out of fear of what the Romans might do to suppress an insurrection, they plotted to have Jesus arrested and put to death.

On that Friday, Jesus, the one his followers believed to be the chosen one to redeem the nation of Israel, was handed over to the Roman authorities by the chief priests and leaders. He was crucified on a cross, dying a horrible death. Understandably, the disciples were filled with grief and sadness. The one in whom they had placed their hopes was now gone. Their dreams for their nation, and no doubt for themselves, were shattered. They were probably wondering, *Where is God in all of this? What will happen now? Why didn't God save him? Does God even exist?* And the response from heaven to these questions appeared to be silence. Where were the stones that were supposed to be crying out? For the disciples, from the moment of his death and in those first few days, no matter what Jesus had told them, all they could hear was the deafening silence of God.

But on the first day of the week everything changed. In the early dawn, a group of women (according to Luke 24:10 it was Mary Magdalene, Joanna, Mary the mother of James, and other women) went to the tomb where Jesus had been buried. But the stone had been rolled away, and two men in dazzling apparel told the women that Jesus was risen. They rushed back and told the eleven disciples and the other followers gathered with them. No one was really sure what to make of this news.

Two of the group, Cleopas and an unnamed disciple, set off on the road to Emmaus, still stunned by all that had happened and still feeling the sting and silence of death. A stranger joined them on the way and engaged them in conversation. As he walked alongside them, he asked questions, listened, encouraged them with the promises of the Scriptures, and challenged them to have faith. Finally, their eyes were open to the presence of Jesus walking with them, made known to them in the breaking of the bread. His presence changed everything and taught them about who God is and what God is all about.

# Jesus Comes Alongside the Broken

The first thing we learn about who God is through this story is that God has a desire to walk alongside the broken and grieving. Have you ever experienced grief? Have you ever felt the sting of death? Have you ever lost someone that you love so dearly that your head is down, you are bent over, and your eyes are filled with tears? Why didn't the men recognize Jesus? Because they were crying. They were broken. They were lost and they were directionless. They didn't know what they were going to do.

You can almost imagine their conversation. "We thought he was going to be the one. We put our faith in him. We thought he was going to save Israel. We thought he was the Messiah, and now all our hope is lost. Why did this have to happen? Why didn't God save him?"

Jesus always shows up among the broken, the lost, the grieving, just as he did that day. At the beginning of his mission, Jesus announced what he was all about—that God had anointed him to bring good news to the poor, proclaim release to the captives, recovery of sight to the blind, and to let the oppressed go free (Luke 4:18).

**(Clayton)** My preaching professor, Dr. Zan Wesley Holmes, Jr., used to challenge people to read the Bible and always be on the lookout for where Jesus shows up. Throughout the Scriptures, we see that God is at work in the broken places of life. Wherever people are struggling. Wherever people are asking the question, "How could God let this happen?" Wherever there is silence. Wherever people have lost their hope. Jesus shows up.

When we are grieving—whether it's the loss of a loved one, the loss of a job, or the loss of a dream—it's so hard for us to have eyes to see how and where Jesus is showing up. Grief is a paralyzing force, and it can happen to any of us. It's no sin to grieve. In fact, the Bible tells us to go ahead and grieve, just not as those who have no hope (1 Thessalonians 4:13). Because Jesus is with us, we can grieve, knowing that death will not have the last word.

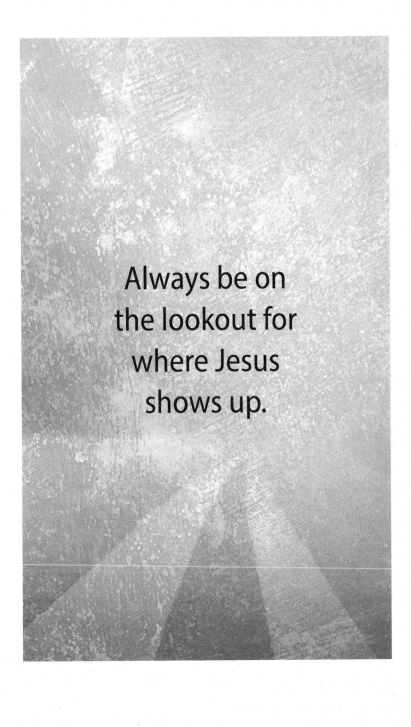

Always be on
the lookout for
where Jesus
shows up.

**Clayton)** My friend Sam played football in high school as a defensive linesman. Once his team was watching the film of the previous game so the coach could critique their performance. On one play, the opposing team's running back made a nice run for a big gain of yardage right through the middle of the defense. The coach growled, "Where were you, Sam?" Sam answered, "I got blocked, Coach." What the coach said next has been a defining philosophy for his life. The coach said, "Well, son, it's no sin to get blocked, but it is a sin to stay blocked!"

God has a way of showing up in our lives when life has blocked us. It is no sin to be blocked or to get blocked. It happens to all of us. But it is a sin to stay in that place and refuse to see that God is with us to help us through those times. Jesus comes along and enters into the conversation even when we don't even recognize that he is with us. He refuses to leave us in that place. Instead, he encourages and challenges us to see that God is at work in the midst of life and death.

# Jesus Encourages the Discouraged

Though they did not recognize the risen Christ with them, Jesus encouraged his followers as they were walking and talking along their journey of grief. He spoke Scriptures and talked about God's promises. He revealed to them that in the life, death, and resurrection of the Messiah, God has promised to give us eternal life. God has promised us that death is not the end of the story.

These disciples had seen Jesus defeated. They had lost their hope. They had followed Jesus because they were drawn to his message of love. They believed he was going to restore the nation. Now everything seemed lost. Jesus chided them for their lack of faith, and then, beginning with Moses and the prophets, he reminded them of the story of God working to save people, all pointing to the Messiah. They would look back on this conversation and say, "Were not our hearts burning within us while he was talking to us on the road, while he was opening the scriptures to us?" (Luke 24:32).

Often our best sight is hindsight. As we go through life, we are often unaware of the many ways God walks with us and encourages us along the journey. When you are going through a particularly difficult stretch of life, it's easy to feel alone, as if no one cares about your situation. But think about where you are today. You didn't get where you are all by yourself. When we look back across the years of our lives, we find that there are many people God has placed along our paths who have given us support and encouragement. While we might not recognize it at the time, looking back our hearts are filled with gratitude for people who stood beside us, gave us a word of advice, believed in us, and challenged us to keep on going forward. As we think in terms of our faith, there are a cloud of witnesses who cheer us on to run the race, staying focused on Jesus (Hebrews 12:1-2). In hindsight, our hearts burn within us, as we remember the way they made the Scriptures come alive through their words and actions.

The challenge for each of us is to do that for others. Having been blessed ourselves by the encouragement of others we have met along the way, we reach out to share that same good news with others. So many people walking the road of life face discouragement and frustration. They need to know that there is a God who understands and who has not given up on them.

**(Clayton)** Several years ago, a young man attending the church I serve got into some real trouble. Struggling with an addiction, he made some really bad decisions and ended up in legal trouble. Several of us from the church visited him while he was in jail and were there in the courtroom when he was sentenced. Many of these same people wrote to him while he served out his sentence, and when he got out, were there to counsel him and encourage him. His journey was not easy, and he had some setbacks along the way, but slowly, as he began to admit his need for help, to trust in God for that help, and to involve himself in a recovery community, something began to happen. A new life began to emerge. Today he is employed in a steady job he has held for several years and is sober, married, and active in his faith through the church. He spends a lot of free time giving encouragement to others in the recovery community. As he said to me, "So many people helped me along the way. It's great to be able to help others." Was his road easy? By no means!

Is it the road to amazing? As he is finding out one day at a time, absolutely!

Perhaps because Cleopas and the other disciple felt so encouraged by the presence and message of their traveling companion, they invited the stranger to stay with them since it was getting late. While everything they had experienced in the stranger's presence had given them encouragement, what happened next would solidify their belief and change them forever. Their mystical encounter with the risen Christ would be recorded by the Gospel writer Luke, and give strength and hope to Christians throughout the ages.

## Jesus Brings New Life

Cleopas and the other disciple stopped for the night after a hard day of traveling on foot. The stranger joined them around a table for a meal. While they were at the table, he took bread, blessed it and broke it, and gave it to them. Where had they seen this before? When Jesus fed the five thousand (Luke 9:16), and when he gathered with his disciples the night before his crucifixion (Luke 22:14-20). Then their eyes were opened, and they recognized that Jesus was with them (Luke 24:31). The same Jesus who had been crucified, who had died and been buried, was now alive with them. He was revealed to them in the breaking of the bread.

What truth did the presence of Christ reveal to them? That the testimony of the women that morning was true—God had raised Jesus, and he was alive! Death's power had been defeated. Jesus had died on Good Friday, but his presence with them now was real. Suddenly he vanished before their eyes and they ran back to Jerusalem to tell the others. There they learned that they were not the only ones to discover the truth that Jesus was alive. Jesus had also appeared to Simon Peter. They shared their story of how Jesus had walked and talked with them along the road to Emmaus, and how he had been made known to them in the breaking of the bread.

Have you ever thought about that when you receive the Lord's Supper, Holy Communion? You gather around the table with other believers, each dealing with his or her own issues. But we are all there, hoping God will be revealed to us in some way. Some of us are bent over by grief and some of us have eyes filled with tears that we don't shed. We haven't been able to see that the risen Christ has been walking with us all along the journey. But Jesus always comes to people who feel lost and broken and who are struggling in life. He always shows up and he brings encouragement. He also opens up the truth about who he is and the promises that he came to show us. He teaches us that not even death can separate us from the love of God in Christ Jesus our Lord (see Romans 8:38-39). His presence in the breaking of the bread reminds us of the power of resurrection.

**(Clayton)** One summer I was serving as a counselor at a senior high youth camp. A seventeen-year-old boy, Max, was part of the camp, and Max was not like the other kids. Max was born with several disabilities, but his parents ensured that, as much as possible, he was able to do what other boys and girls did. Far beyond what anyone imagined was possible for him, Max participated fully in school, in church, and in life. It was a delight to have him as a part of the camp that week, and the other kids were so great about including and encouraging him.

The last night of the camp we served Communion as part of our closing worship service. After recalling all that God had done for us, we broke the bread and gave thanks over the cup, and people began to come forward to receive. With the most sincere eyes, Max approached me and asked, "Am I worthy to have Communion?" I looked at this wonderful young man and said, "Max, because of God's grace you are worthy, and I am worthy, and all of us are worthy." I remember watching that young man with a contagious smile, walking forward to receive Communion, saying over and over, "Thank you, Jesus, I am worthy!"

When we gather around the Lord's Table, amazing things happen. Grace is revealed. God's power of resurrection becomes more than a concept, and it is a force unleashed in our lives. The road to amazing tells us there is a love that you can nail to a tree and bury in a tomb, but it will never die. The stones will cry out. The same God who raised his Son, Jesus Christ, will raise us up with him also—nothing can ever separate us from this great love.

We are resurrection people. We recognize and experience the realities of death in this world, but we know there is more to the story. God is not finished with us. God is at work to bring new life and new hope into our lives.

**(Mary Brooke)** As Clayton has noted, our family endured a heart-breaking tragedy with the untimely death of our younger brother, Kelley. In Kelley's final weeks, I asked for some time off from my job to spend time with him and my family. My supervisor, Bishop John L. Hopkins, graciously granted my request. He added a pastoral word: "Look for the ways God shows up." As I was driving down a country road to the small Texas town where our brother lived, I suddenly saw thousands of small butterflies fluttering across the countryside. Remembering that butterflies are a symbol of resurrection, I felt God was indeed "showing up," reminding me of God's presence on this difficult journey.

God continued to "show up" throughout that time in many different ways, especially through the prayers and presence of friends and family. I felt that I was literally picked up by the church—the body of Christ—and carried through this period of grief and sorrow. Since that time, I've tried to make it a daily practice to "look for the ways God shows up." For in doing so, "the road to Emmaus" turns into "the road to amazing."

We are
resurrection people.
We recognize and
experience the
realities of death
in this world,
but we know there
is more to the story.

Have you experienced the many ways God shows up? It doesn't always happen on our schedule or when it is convenient for us. But sometimes our eyes are opened and we begin to see what makes the journey of faith so amazing: God is with us. We are not alone. And as we begin to recognize God's presence and actively look for it in our daily living, we begin to recognize who is with us on the journey.

God, revealed in Jesus the Christ, is with us to comfort us, to encourage us, and to reveal God's power of resurrection and new life. This happened on the road to Emmaus long ago. And it is happening every day as we learn to trust God on the road to amazing!

*God of resurrection and new life, thank you for the assurance that death is not the end of life. Just as you raised your Son, Jesus, remind me that you have promised to raise me up also. Remind me, Lord, that the promise of resurrection is not just after we die. You are present with me now. Open my eyes to see you and to find strength and encouragement from you. In my daily life, help me to know you are walking alongside me. Give me the courage to step out in faith and do for others what you have done for me. When all hope seems lost, give me the voice to cry out that you are alive and that nothing can separate us from your love. Thank you, Lord, for this road of faith that truly is amazing. In Jesus' name. Amen.*

# REFLECT

## ▓ Historical Marker

Reread Luke 24:13-35 ( see pages 86–87).

The Road to Emmaus story is found only in the book of Luke, although it likely existed in oral tradition prior to the writing of the Gospel. In fact, Mark's Gospel seems to reference it in Mark 16:12–13, which is a short version of this story (typical of Mark). Cleopas and his unnamed companion are walking to the village of Emmaus, about seven miles from Jerusalem when a stranger joins them. It was the resurrected Jesus, but their eyes were kept from recognizing him. Did God keep them from recognizing Jesus? Or was this more about their condition they were in, finding themselves downcast in grief?

Jesus listens to their story, and then chides them for their lack of faith. He opens the Scriptures to them and, beginning with Moses and all the prophets, he interprets the Scriptures for them. For Luke, this is a key theme: Jesus is the culmination and centerpiece of the salvation history that God began among the Hebrew people long ago. In Jesus, this covenant relationship is now fulfilled and expanded to all the world.

At the close of the day, the men are nearing their destination, and Jesus (the stranger) appears to be traveling on. They implore him to stay with them. As they sit down to eat a meal, Jesus takes the bread, blesses it, breaks it, and gives it to them. It is in the breaking of the bread that their eyes are opened and they recognize him. He had been with them all day, but until this moment they did not know who he was. As they run back to tell the others, they reflect on how their hearts burned when he was with them on the road.

How often we look back and see that Jesus was with us all along our journey and we did not realize it!

Where has Jesus surprised you by "showing up" on your faith journey?

# ☞ **Points of Interest**

What insights did you gain from each section of this chapter?

The Road to Amazing

Jesus Comes Alongside the Broken

Jesus Encourages the Discouraged

Jesus Brings New Life

 **Souvenir**

What "souvenir" will you take with you as a remembrance of this chapter?

# NOTES

## Chapter 1: Baptism: The Journey Begins

1. Jan Milic Lochman, *The Faith We Confess*, trans. David Lewis (Philadelphia: Fortress Press, 1984), 220.
2. Layton De Vries. "Child of God," (Dallas, TX: Choristers Guild, 2011).
3. *Baptismal Covenant II-B, The United Methodist Book of Worship*, (Nashville: Abingdon, 1992), 104.
4. Merriam-Webster.com, s.v. "Become," accessed October 28, 2015, http://www.merriam-webster .com/dictionary/become.
5. *Baptismal Covenant II-B*, 105.

## Chapter 2: Defining Moments on the Journey

1. "A Covenant Prayer in the Wesleyan Tradition," *The United Methodist Hymnal* (Nashville: The United Methodist Publishing House, 1989), 607.

2. "Luke," Professor J.A. Findlay, *The Abingdon Bible Commentary* (Garden City, NY: Doubleday & Company, Inc., 1929, 1957), 1041.
3. William Arndt, F. Wilbur Gingrich, Frederick W. Danker, and Walter Bauer. *A Greek-English Lexicon of the New Testament and Other Early Christian Literature: A Translation and Adaptation of the Fourth Revised and Augmented Edition of Walter Bauer's Griechisch-Deutsches Wörterbuch Zu Den Schriften Des Neuen Testaments Und Der Übrigen Urchristlichen Literatur.* (Chicago: University of Chicago Press, 1979), 764.
4. Findlay, *The Abingdon Bible Commentary*, 1041.
5. This story originally appeared as an online article: "Pastor's civil rights work still matters," Mary Brooke Casad, *United Methodist News Service*, February 28, 2012, http://www.umc.org/news-and -media/pastors-civil-rights-work-still-matters.

**Chapter 3: Transforming Journey**

1. Jonathan Larson, "Seasons of Love," in *Rent* (Santa Monica, CA: Universal Music Publishing Group, 1996).

# ACKNOWLEDGMENTS

**(Clayton)** So many people have helped give shape to the formulation of this material. Writing with my sister, Mary Brooke Casad, has been and continues to be a joyous experience. She is one of the most creative, dedicated people I know; a person who truly strives to live her faith in word and deed. Many of the stories we use to illustrate the Scriptures in The Basics series come out of our family experiences in both joyful and trying times. You are a blessing!

I'm grateful to the Worship Team and staff of First United Methodist Church, Richardson, Texas, who helped develop the sermon series in which some of these messages originally appeared, and the congregation who first heard these messages and gave good feedback. Jennifer Rawlinson and Drew Presley were helpful early on in the process with sermon transcriptions. I am always thankful for the many mentors who have blessed my life, particularly my preaching mentor, Dr. Don Benton, and preaching professor, Dr. Zan W. Holmes, Jr.

My wife, Lori, and children, Erin, Katy, and Grant, continue to bring so much joy to my life. They have put up with my writing and offered gracious feedback as well as constant encouragement and support. Thank you all for blessing my life!

**(Mary Brooke)** I'm profoundly grateful for the opportunity to coauthor The Basics series with Clayton, who besides being my biological brother is a true brother in Christ. His genuine faith is lived out authentically in every aspect of his life, bringing blessing and joy to me and to many others. Thank you, Clayton!

Our stories reflect the blessings of family, friends, and communities of faith who have enriched and shaped us. Except for our family members, the names of other persons in our stories have been changed. I give thanks to God for all who have been a part of my faith journey.

With gratitude for their support, encouragement, and love, I offer my heartfelt thanks to my husband, Vic, and our family: Carter, McCrae, Melissa, Revol, Patrick, and Ana. (And a special word of thanks to McCrae for assisting with the transcriptions of his uncle's sermons!)

We both gratefully acknowledge Neil Alexander and the wonderful folks at The United Methodist Publishing House. A special word of appreciation goes to Susan Salley and Sally Sharpe. Thank you!